Designed by Nature

Clothing

Wendy Hinote Lanier
and John Willis

MEDIA ENHANCED BOOKS
AV2 BY WEIGL
ADDED VALUE • AUDIO VISUAL
www.av2books.com

Go to www.av2books.com, and enter this book's unique code.

BOOK CODE

AVB45757

AV² by Weigl brings you media enhanced books that support active learning.

AV² provides enriched content that supplements and complements this book. Weigl's AV² books strive to create inspired learning and engage young minds in a total learning experience.

Your AV² Media Enhanced books come alive with...

Audio
Listen to sections of the book read aloud.

Key Words
Study vocabulary, and complete a matching word activity.

Video
Watch informative video clips.

Quizzes
Test your knowledge.

Embedded Weblinks
Gain additional information for research.

Slide Show
View images and captions, and prepare a presentation.

Try This!
Complete activities and hands-on experiments.

... and much, much more!

Published by AV² by Weigl
350 5th Avenue, 59th Floor
New York, NY 10118
Website: www.av2books.com

Library of Congress Cataloging-in-Publication Data
Names: Lanier, Wendy Hinote, author. | Willis, John, author.
Title: Clothing / Wendy Hinote Lanier, John Willis.
Other titles: Clothing inspired by nature
Description: New York, NY : AV2 by Weigl, [2019] | Series: Designed by nature | Previous title: Clothing inspired by nature. | Audience: Grades 4 to 6. | Includes index.
Identifiers: LCCN 2018053539 (print) | LCCN 2018057245 (ebook) | ISBN 9781489697028 (Multi User Ebook) | ISBN 9781489697042 (Single User Ebook) | ISBN 9781489697011 (hardcover : alk. paper) | ISBN 9781489697035 (softcover : alk. paper)
Subjects: LCSH: Clothing trade--Juvenile literature. | Protective clothing--Juvenile literature. | Discoveries in science--Juvenile literature.
Classification: LCC HD9940.A2 (ebook) | LCC HD9940.A2 L3625 2019 (print) | DDC 338.4/7687--dc23
LC record available at https://lccn.loc.gov/2018053539

Printed in the United States of America in Brainerd, Minnesota
1 2 3 4 5 6 7 8 9 0 22 21 20 19 18

122018
102318

Project Coordinator: John Willis   Designer: Ana María Vidal

Every reasonable effort has been made to trace ownership and to obtain permission to reprint copyright material. The publishers would be pleased to have any errors or omissions brought to their attention so that they may be corrected in subsequent printings.

Weigl acknowledges Alamy, Getty Images, and iStock as its primary image suppliers for this title.

First published by North Star Editions in 2019

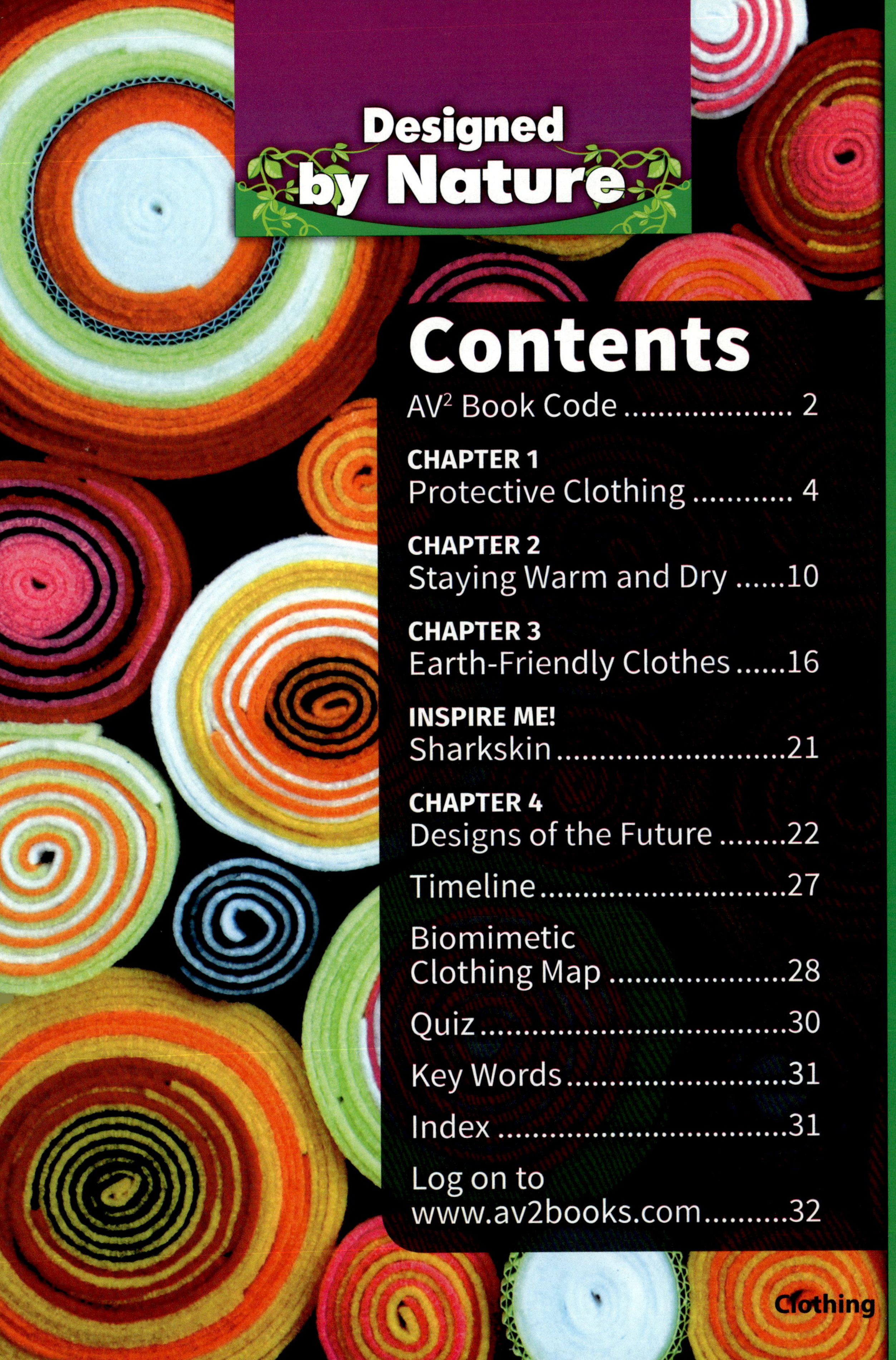

Contents

Chapter 1

Firefighters wear flame-resistant clothing to prevent burns.

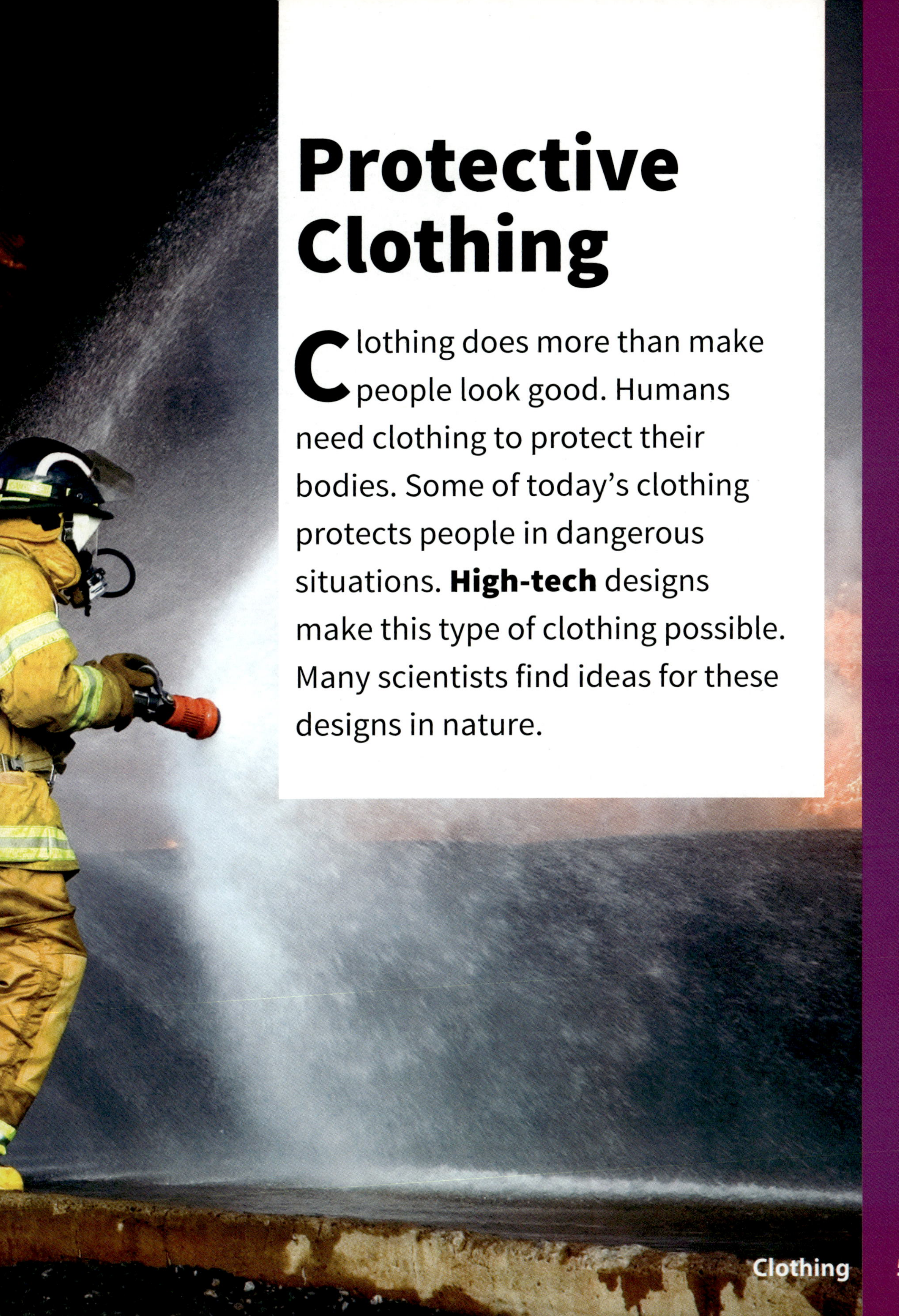

Protective Clothing

Clothing does more than make people look good. Humans need clothing to protect their bodies. Some of today's clothing protects people in dangerous situations. **High-tech** designs make this type of clothing possible. Many scientists find ideas for these designs in nature.

Spider silk can be stretched several times its length without breaking.

Scientists identify a problem. Then they study how plants or animals solve it. They make inventions that copy these solutions. This process is called biomimicry.

Biomimicry is responsible for some of the newest protective clothing. For example, police officers and soldiers use body armor to stay safe. But most armor is tough and inflexible. Researchers turned to spider silk to solve this problem. Spider silk is one of the strongest fibers in nature. One company is using spider silk to make a new kind of body armor.

Some spiders can create **seven different** kinds of silk.

A strand of spider silk circling Earth would weigh about **1 pound**. (0.45 kilograms)

Some kinds of **spider silk** can be stretched **two to five** times their length before breaking.

Unfortunately, it can be difficult to produce large amounts of spider silk. Spiders do not work well in groups. So, researchers decided to put spider **DNA** into silkworms. The silkworms then make large amounts of silk fibers. These fibers are similar to spider silk. Using the silk fibers, researchers created a strong cloth known as Dragon Silk. This material can be used to make protective clothing. The U.S. Army hired the creators of Dragon Silk. The Army wanted them to design body armor for soldiers.

A Sticky Idea

A famous example of biomimicry is Velcro. In 1948, a Swiss inventor returned from a hike with seed burrs stuck to his clothes. When he looked closely, he saw the burrs had tiny hooks. The hooks had caught on the loops in his clothes. He made two kinds of cloth inspired by the burrs. One cloth had hooks. The other had loops. The two fabrics attached together firmly. It took eight years to perfect the design.

Nature is also inspiring new kinds of flame-resistant materials. For example, researchers have developed a new coating for cloth. It is a mixture of clay, fish DNA, and a substance found in lobster shells. The coating is applied in layers. It keeps clothing safe from fire. And it is even **eco-friendly**.

Chapter 2

Advanced clothing technology allows athletes to train and compete in cold weather.

Staying Warm and Dry

Clothing can protect people in extreme weather. One example is a jacket inspired by penguins. Many penguins hunt in freezing water. Their feathers keep them warm. At the bottom of each feather is a muscle. In water, the muscle pulls the feather down so it lies flat. This gives the penguin a smooth, waterproof coat. On land, the muscles relax. When this happens, the feathers form a thick coat filled with air. This protects the penguin against wind.

An **insert** for jackets mimics penguin feathers. The insert is made of two layers of fabric. Strips of fabric connect the two layers. When the strips stand up straight, the jacket fills with air. When the strips lie flat, the jacket becomes thin and tight. The insert protects people in wet, cold, and windy weather.

In Antarctica, penguins swim in waters as cold as 29 degrees Fahrenheit (–2 degrees Celsius).

Even in cold weather, exercise causes people to sweat. The moisture under their clothes can make them feel cold. To solve this problem, researchers are inventing clothing that releases moisture. This new type of fabric was inspired by plants.

A Smart Scarf

In 2011, a designer created a new type of scarf. It was based on a hornbeam leaf. Hornbeam leaves have closed folds. When the leaves pop out of their buds, the folds open. The wool scarf folds into a small package, much like a hornbeam leaf. It can fit inside a pocket or purse. When opened, the scarf creates a large, warm wrap for the neck.

Many companies are using advanced technology to make waterproof clothing.

Plants give off extra water through a process called transpiration. During transpiration, small openings in leaves release water and oxygen. One clothing company makes outerwear inspired by this process. In cold weather, the fabric's fibers stay closed. This keeps water out. But when the person's body warms, the fibers open. Heat and sweat can escape.

Another type of outerwear is inspired by the lotus plant. Lotus leaves are covered with tiny bumps and a waxy material. This surface allows water to bead up and roll off. Meanwhile, the water carries away dust and dirt.

By studying lotus plants, researchers found a new way of making waterproof clothing. They did this by applying special coatings to fabric. These coatings create a slick surface with tiny bumps. The fabric then mimics the surface of a lotus leaf. It stops water from soaking into the fibers. Instead, the water slides right off.

Chapter 3

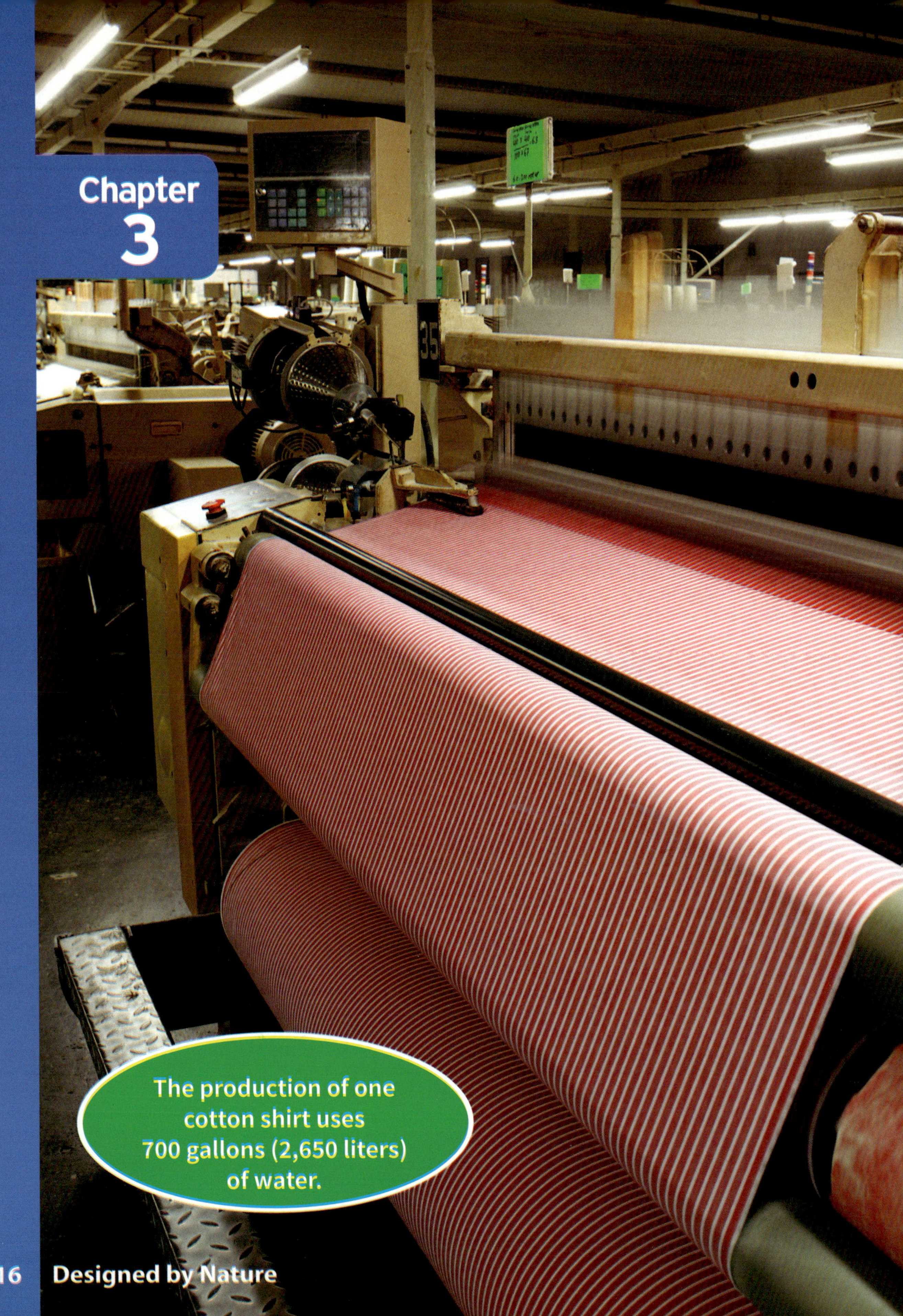

The production of one cotton shirt uses 700 gallons (2,650 liters) of water.

Earth-Friendly Clothes

Making colorful fabrics is often harmful to the environment. The process uses large amounts of water, energy, and dyes. Most dyes are made using chemicals. Sometimes, these chemicals end up in rivers and streams. They can also harm the people who work with them.

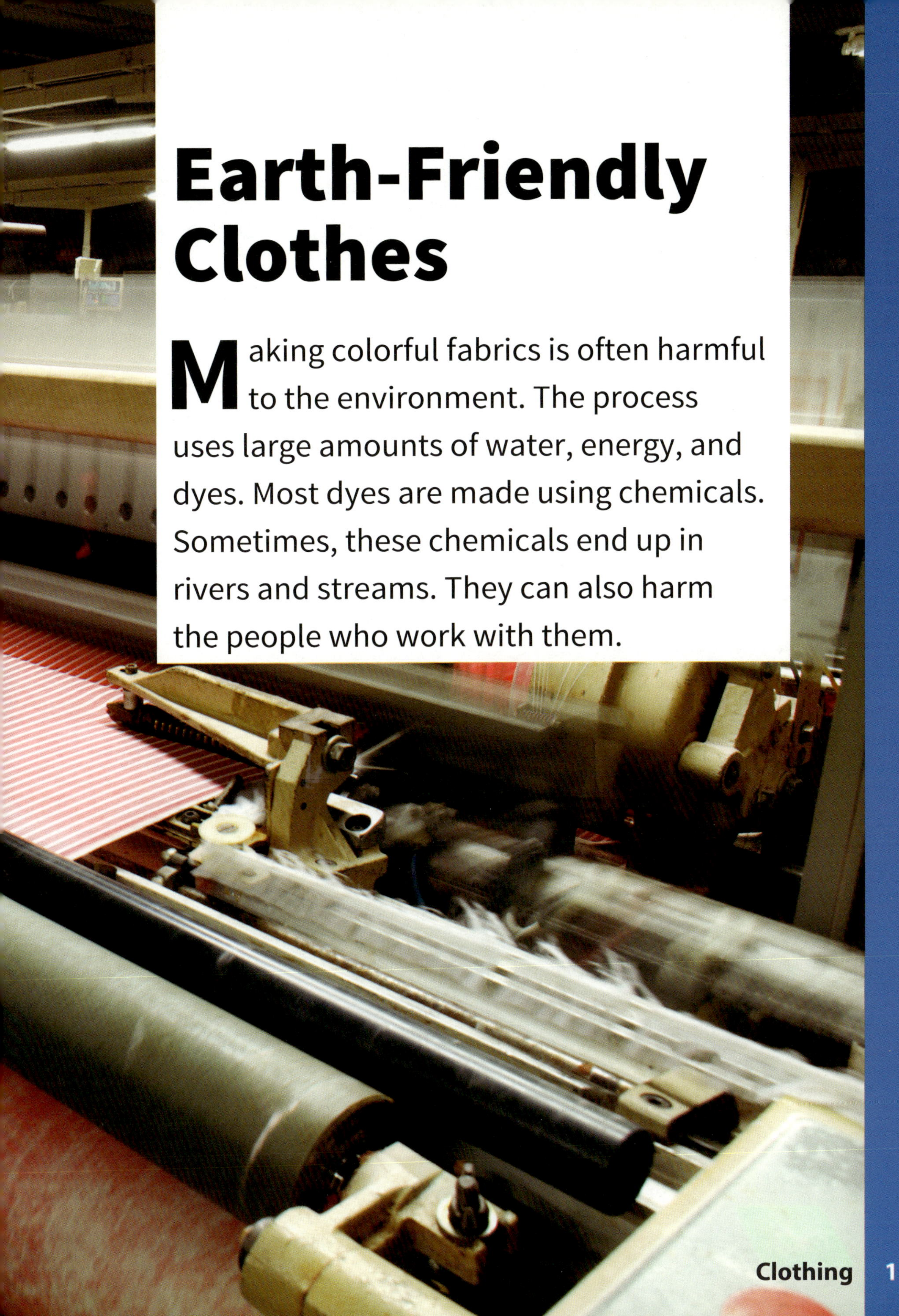

The morpho butterfly has inspired a dye-free cloth. Morpho butterflies are bright blue. Their color is the result of tiny, overlapping scales. These scales produce color by bending, absorbing, and reflecting light.

Morpho butterflies can have wingspans of up to 8 inches (20 centimeters).

Morphotex is a cloth inspired by the morpho butterfly. This cloth produces color in a similar way. Unlike most clothing, it does not use dye. Instead, the cloth's fibers are arranged in layers. The fibers interact with light, similar to the butterfly's scales.

The thickness of the layers changes the color of the cloth. Morphotex can be red, green, blue, or violet. The idea behind Morphotex has also been used on electronic screens.

Creating Color

Morpho butterfly scales interact with sunlight to produce shades of blue.

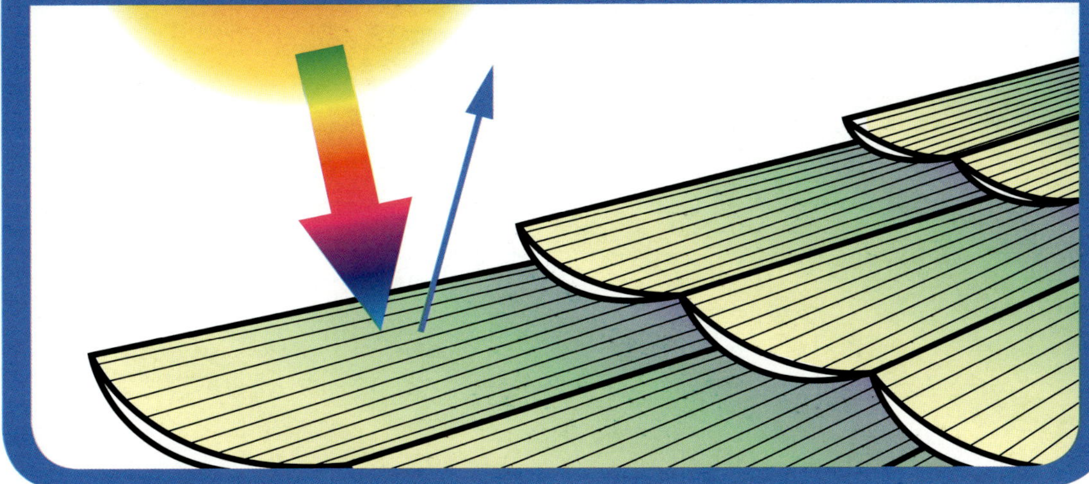

Some designers are using natural materials to grow eco-friendly fabric. One designer was inspired by kombucha. This is a drink made from **bacteria**, **yeast**, and sweet tea. The bacteria and yeast cause a chemical change in the tea. As a result, a substance called cellulose forms on the drink. The designer uses a similar process to grow large sheets of cellulose. When the sheets dry, they form a leathery material. She uses this material to make dresses, jackets, and even shoes.

Nature inspired another designer to make an eco-friendly coat. The designer tucked seeds into the coat's wool fibers. When winter is over, the coat can be planted. The wool acts as fertilizer. In summer, the seeds grow into food.

Pollination Stations

Bees spread pollen when they land on flowers. This process allows more plants to grow. But in recent years, many bees have been dying. Bee populations are especially low in cities. To help solve this problem, one designer created bee-friendly clothing. She covered cloth with a nectar-like mixture. She also added images of plant pollen. When hung or worn outside, the clothing attracts bees.

Inspire Me!

Sharkskin

Sharks are inspiring new technologies in clothing. Sharkskin is made up of flexible layers of small, tooth-like structures. As a shark swims, these "teeth" direct water over the shark's body. This allows for swift, easy movement. It also keeps organisms such as algae from clinging to the shark.

A new clothing product acts similarly to sharkskin. In 2000, Speedo introduced swimwear called Fastskin. Fastskin is a stretchy material with a surface of V-shaped ridges. The ridges were based on the tooth-like structures of sharkskin. The full Fastskin suit first appeared at the 2000 Olympics.

Many Olympians who wore Fastskin suits won medals. It is unclear whether the suits' ridged surface helped lead to their success. Still, Olympic officials decided that Fastskin might work too well. The material was banned from Olympic competition in 2009.

In 2009, athletes wearing Fastskin broke more than 43 world swimming records at a world championship in Rome, Italy.

Chapter 4

Nature will continue to influence protective, outdoor, and everyday clothing.

Designs of the Future

Nature is inspiring scientists to solve challenging problems in new ways. Nature-inspired clothing protects people in the outdoors. It can also benefit the environment. However, creating new products takes time. Many clothing designs are still in the early stages.

One possible design features **artificial** muscles. Scientists studied muscles in animals, including octopus legs and elephant trunks. Then they recreated the muscles out of tiny **carbon** tubes. They hope to use the muscles in clothing for older people. Older people often have weak muscles. The new clothing could give them more strength. This would help people stay active as they age.

Scientists are also working on new types of **camouflage**. They are studying squids for inspiration. Squids have color-changing cells just below their skin. When they expand or contract the cells, their color changes. This allows squids to blend in with their surroundings. Scientists hope to create clothing that works in a similar way. This technology could be especially useful to the military.

Squids have also inspired self-repairing clothing. Squids use suckers to grab their prey. These suckers contain sharp teeth. **Proteins** from the teeth are strong and flexible. Scientists are recreating this protein to make cloth that repairs itself. They do this by covering the cloth with a coating of the protein. If the cloth rips, they simply add water. The proteins then spread toward the rip. This reconnects the torn fabric. Scientists hope to use self-repairing cloth in everyday clothing. In the future, a liquid form of the protein might be available. The liquid would help clothes repair while they are washed.

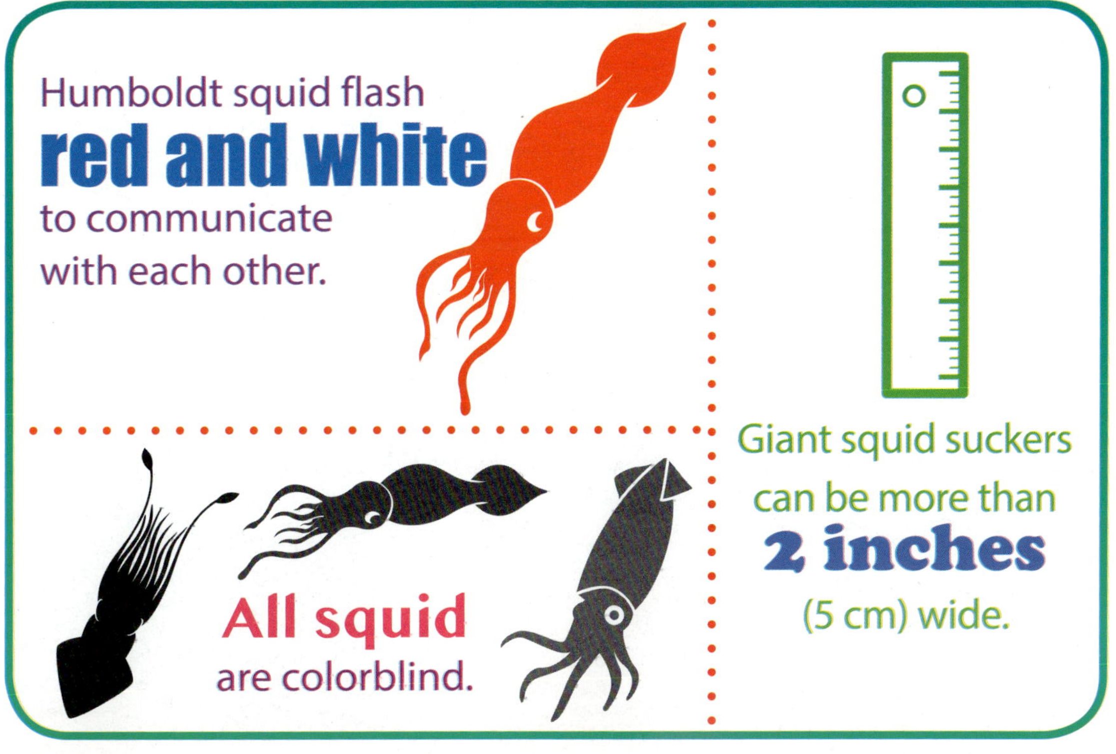

Nature is a source of inspiration for many kinds of technology. And clothing is no exception. Thanks to nature, scientists are changing the world of fashion.

Modern technology helps scientists observe nature more closely. One example is advanced microscopes. New tools like these will lead to even more nature-inspired inventions.

In the future, a liquid form of protein could fix ripped clothes.

Timeline

Although the word biomimetics is fairly new, humans have been using nature to inspire clothing for thousands of years. Today, new developments make clothing safer and more effective.

3500 BC People in China begin to use silkworms for their silk.

1948 AD Inspired by burrs, Swiss inventor George de Mestral creates Velcro.

1969 The term biomimetics is first used by biophysicist and inventor Otto Schmitt.

2000 Olympic swimmers wearing Fastskin swimwear set 13 world records.

2012 A University of Massachusetts research team develops a very strong adhesive material, based on gecko feet, that is partly made from special fabrics.

2016 Inspired by squid, scientists develop a solution, made of bacteria and yeast, that can be used to repair many kinds of fabrics.

Biomimetic Clothing Map

Pacific Ocean

North America

Atlantic Ocean

South America

People often look for natural solutions when creating new kinds of clothing. Today, new wearable inventions inspired by nature are being created, developed, and sold around the world.

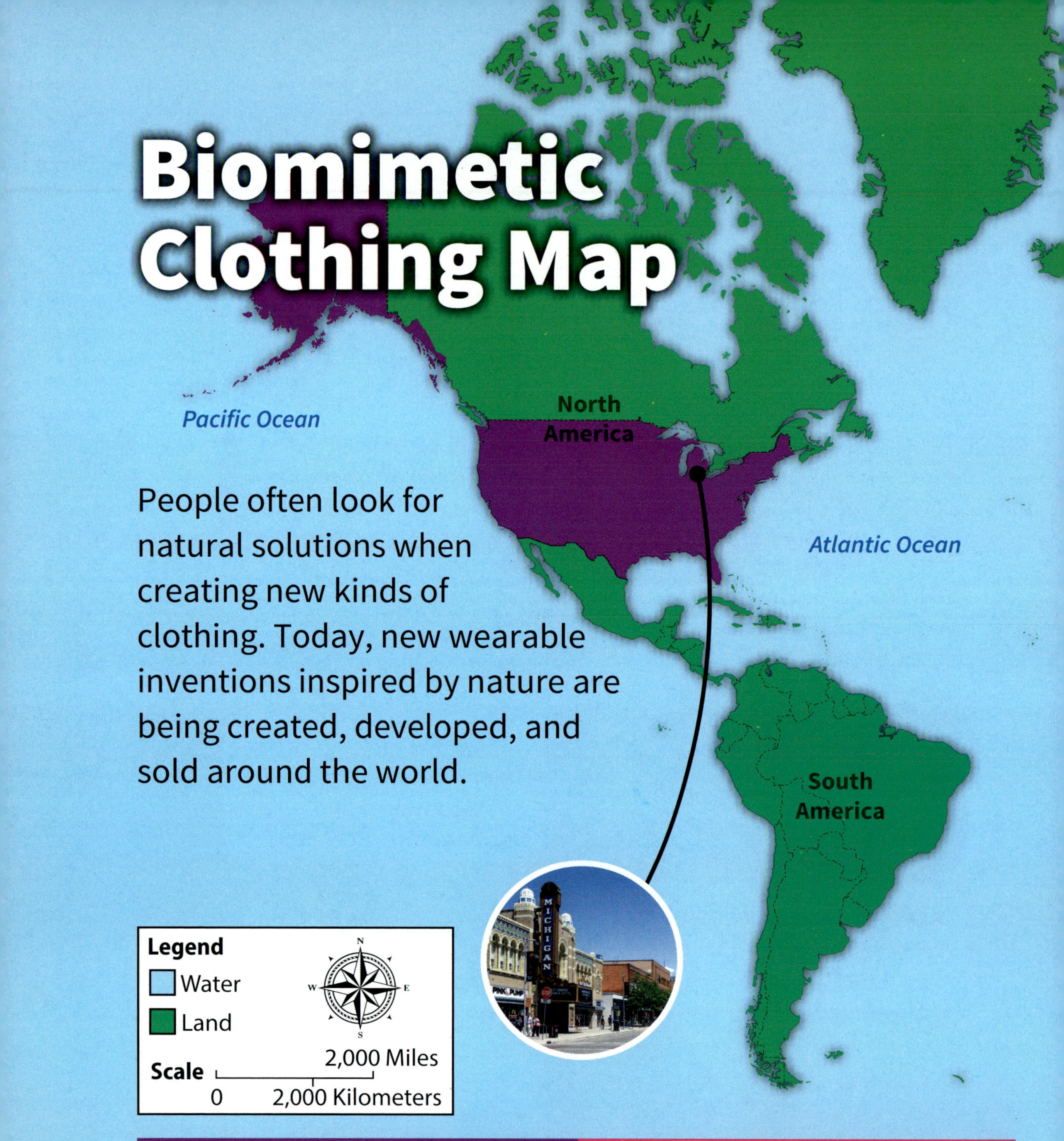

Legend

Water

Land

Scale 0 2,000 Miles 2,000 Kilometers

United States

Located in Ann Arbor, Michigan, Kraig Biocraft Laboratories creates products using spider silk. In 2016, it was awarded a contract with the U.S. Army to develop new forms of protective gear.

Great Britain

Swiss inventor George de Mestral named Velcro by combining French words meaning "velvet" and "hook." Today, Velcro has offices in many locations, including Middlewich, Great Britain.

Turkey

In 2003, researchers at Kocaeli University, in Kocaeli, Turkey, examined how lotus leaves repel water and developed a waterproof coating.

Australia

Founded near Australia's Bondi Beach, Speedo is an Australian swimwear company responsible for many innovative designs, including Fastskin.

Quiz

1 What happens during transpiration?

Answer: Small openings in leaves release water and oxygen

2 When did people in China first domesticate silkworms?

Answer: 3500 BC

3 What is kombucha made of?

Answer: Bacteria, yeast, and sweet tea

4 What insect inspired a dye-free cloth?

Answer: The morpho butterfly

5 What is sharkskin covered with?

Answer: Small, tooth-like structures

6 What did George de Mestral invent?

Answer: Velcro

7 How wide can a giant squid sucker be?

Answer: More than 2 inches (5 cm)

8 What materials can be used to create artificial muscles?

Answer: Carbon tubes

9 What are lotus leaves covered with?

Answer: Tiny bumps and a waxy material

10 How much water is used to produce one cotton shirt?

Answer: 700 gallons (2,650 L)

Key Words

artificial: made by humans instead of occurring naturally

bacteria: single-celled living things. They can be useful or harmful.

camouflage: a pattern that is designed to look like its surroundings

carbon: one of the basic chemical elements of all living things

DNA: the genetic material in the cells of living organisms

eco-friendly: not harmful to the environment

high-tech: using advanced technology

insert: an object that is placed inside another object

proteins: molecules that are important in telling a living cell what to do

yeast: a type of fungus used to make foods and drinks, such as bread

Index

Log on to www.av2books.com

AV² by Weigl brings you media enhanced books that support active learning. Go to www.av2books.com, and enter the special code found on page 2 of this book. You will gain access to enriched and enhanced content that supplements and complements this book. Content includes video, audio, weblinks, quizzes, a slide show, and activities.

AV² Online Navigation

Audio
Listen to sections of the book read aloud.

Book Pages
AV² pages directly correspond to pages in the book.

Video
Watch informative video clips.

Embedded Weblinks
Gain additional information for research.

Key Words
Study vocabulary, and complete a matching word activity.

Try This!
Complete activities and hands-on experiments.

Quizzes
Test your knowledge.

Slide Show
View images and captions, and prepare a presentation.

AV² was built to bridge the gap between print and digital. We encourage you to tell us what you like and what you want to see in the future.

Sign up to be an AV² Ambassador at www.av2books.com/ambassador.

Due to the dynamic nature of the Internet, some of the URLs and activities provided as part of AV² by Weigl may have changed or ceased to exist. AV² by Weigl accepts no responsibility for any such changes. All media enhanced books are regularly monitored to update addresses and sites in a timely manner. Contact AV² by Weigl at 1-866-649-3445 or av2books@weigl.com with any questions, comments, or feedback.